D1319845

MEANINGFUL
COACHING

SDI in Coaching

Tina Mertel M.A., A.C.C.

PERSONAL
STRENGTHS
PUBLISHING

Copyright © 2010 Personal Strengths Publishing®, Inc.

All rights reserved in the U.S.A., and worldwide. No part of this publication may be reproduced, stored in a retrieval system or transmitted in any form or by any means, electronic, mechanical, photocopying, recording or otherwise, without prior written permission from the publisher.

ISBN: 978-1-932627-10-7

For ease of reading, the U.S. registration symbol (®), the copyright symbol (©), or the marketing symbol (™) sometimes are omitted. Publications, trademarks and trade names are the intellectual property of Personal Strengths Publishing, Inc. and may not be reproduced or adapted in any way. Each of our publications is protected by international copyright law with all rights reserved. Trademarks and trade names are registered internationally and may not be used without the express written consent of Personal Strengths Publishing, Inc. We offer a reward for any information leading to recovery of damages due to copyright violation.

Published by Personal Strengths Publishing, Inc.
P.O. Box 2605 Carlsbad, CA 92018-2605
1-800-624-7347
www.personalstrengths.com

Printed in the United States of America

TABLE OF CONTENTS

PREFACE:

In The Practice of Coaching   13

CHAPTER 1:

The Purpose of Coaching   15

CHAPTER 2:

The International Coach Federation   25

CHAPTER 3:

Introduction to the Strength

Deployment Inventory   39

CHAPTER 4:

Know Thyself   47

CHAPTER 5:

Each Competency Explored   55

CHAPTER 6:

Creating Meaning for Your Client   63

CHAPTER 7:

Blocks Happen   71

CHAPTER 8:

Putting it All Together -
Stories of Coaching to Clients' Values   81

IN CONCLUSION: 93

APPENDIX A:

The 7 Motivational Value Systems   96
Understanding Conflict   97
Strength Management Card   98

APPENDIX B:

Client Preparation Sheet   100

REFERENCES   103

ACKNOWLEDGEMENTS

I'd like to give special acknowledgment to two learning organizations: to Personal Strengths Publishing, Inc. and the works of Dr. Elias H. Porter, and to Accomplishment Coaching where I learned the fundamentals of coaching and the ICF core competencies.

I am grateful to reviewers of this book for both the time they spent and the ideas shared: Carol Brill, Andy Churgin, Donna Maisch, Sheila Legon, Marjorie Busse, and Kim Hay. Thank you to Tim Scudder and Kent Mitchell for partnership in editing and publishing.

This book is dedicated to all those
who have the courage to coach and be coached.

*"Awareness of values
can only enrich a person.
In fact, this inner enrichment
constitutes the meaning of his life."*

–Viktor Frankl, The Doctor and The Soul (1986)

The Practice of Coaching

In the practice of coaching, creating awareness is a core competency. The intention of this book is to create awareness for you, the reader. Creating awareness, coupled with designing actions leads to goal achievement and success. Therefore this book has several workbook pages and areas for reflection so that you reach your goal of being a better coach.

During my coaching education with an ICF-accredited school, I noticed that my fellow coaches performed well at certain competencies, but were weaker in others. I wondered what caused this to occur. In my work with a values-based instrument, I have seen how one's values act as a filter in what one perceives and communicates.

To couple knowledge of the International Coach Federation core competencies with the knowledge of human values is to integrate a coaching methodology with a relationship methodology. These are two powerful means to supporting a client and the core focus of this book.

This book is structured in building blocks. First, your role as a coach is addressed, followed by an overview of the ICF core competencies. An inventory is introduced, where you have the opportunity to identify your own values. With this knowledge, the competencies are again reviewed to reveal your value biases on those competencies. The inventory also assists you in identifying the values of your client so you can create a better rapport and relationship. Possible blocks are noted before the book concludes with client stories showing how these building blocks work together.

With thanks to the International Coach Federation and Personal Strengths Publishing, you are about to heighten your awareness and knowledge — and create a meaningful experience for your clients (whether they be external or internal).

Viktor Frankl in his book, *The Doctor and The Soul* writes, "Awareness of values can only enrich a person. In fact, this inner enrichment constitutes the meaning of his life." (Frankl, 1986). Congratulations on your willingness to explore your effectiveness as coach so that others not only meet their goals, but find their sense of meaning in the process.

— Tina Mertel

CHAPTER 1

THE
PURPOSE
OF COACHING

Clients want to create an end state that they envision. They've tried their own means, but were not successful. They are choosing you as their coach to make it there. The good news is your client has a sense they can get there, otherwise they'd pack up shop and call it quits. They are not seeking a cure or a *healing*. Much like sports coaching, they want to work with someone who spots non-supportive behaviors and supports actions that get to that desired end state. In today's world of readily available information, people are not seeking informational experts – they are seeking support of a different nature – to be held accountable for what they know is possible, yet are stuck in making it happen.

As a coach, you may need to help your client define that *end state*. Too often clients are unclear about what they want. You will hear, "I want a better position," or "I want a richer life." Your coaching will assist them in getting specific. One of the best ways to do this is through applying a form of measurement. Ask your client, how they will know they've reached that end state in a measurable form? Examples include: "I will make $25,000 more by the end of this year," or "I will spend 10 hours per week on my favorite three hobbies starting next month."

You may have a tendency to judge or assess your client's goal. It's not up to you to judge or assess. It is your duty to see that it is measurable and achievable, and to ask the coaching questions that ensure the client sees it this way. If you have an ethical concern or have a dual relationship with the client (such as coaching a friend or relative) or simply are too close to the subject matter (such as you want the same job as your client is going after), then ask yourself if it truly serves your coaching relationship for you to remain the coach.

Coaching is a service designed to support the client's desires. Can you coach to something you don't *agree* with? Only you will know. If you are unsure, an exercise you can use is to rate your disagreement on a scale of 1 to 10 with 1 being a minor disagreement, and 10 being a major disagreement. At level of 4 and above, talk to your own coach to ensure you are detached and continue, or simply refer your client to another coach.

Just as a sports coach must observe an athlete to coach, you must listen to your client to coach. Your client's sense of trust is heightened when you listen well. Sometimes clients don't realize that what they say or how they say it is actually blocking them either intra-personally or interpersonally. For example, a client saying, "I've never been able to do that," often creates a mind-made obstacle. Perhaps it's true they haven't done it to date, but do they give it as a reason not to in the future? Your listening can reveal unconscious patterns that hold them back. Putting the client *at choice* for how they communicate with themselves and others can be a turning point.

Most coaching interactions are held as ongoing sessions. There may be times when you assist a colleague with a few coaching questions or even in a group meeting as a one-time event. The question, "What is our desired end state?" can help to corral a group's focus. But inherent in coaching are follow-up sessions to manage the progress and accountability of the insight gained from a previous session. Your role as coach is to hold the client accountable for their actions both in a coaching session and between appointments. Although at times the client may argue or defend their rights not to be accountable, your mirroring of their choices continues to leave the client *at choice* for the living of their lives.

Much like learning theory, reviewing newly-learned content cements new ways of being and behaving. Popular opinion states that it takes 21 days of repetition for a new habit to form. Having multiple coaching sessions supports the accountability of creating new habits. A client may try to postpone sessions or even be a no-show because his current habits are too strong in the moment. This may be a good place to add a reward or a consequence if the client shows resistance. Your job as coach is to reflect these dynamics and remind them of their desired end state.

Another reason people want to work with coaches is to learn about what gets in their way. There will be times when it most serves the client for you to be simple and direct. An example of this might be when a client is reciting why something is difficult for them to achieve. A simple, direct reflection is to say, "I'd like to draw your attention to the excuses you are giving in this moment. What do you notice?" For you to develop a menu of coaching styles is in your favor. What may be uncomfortable for one coach, could be easy for another. As we support clients in building new muscles, we too as coaches need to develop our weak muscles. It may be that silence is uncomfortable for you, yet silence may be exactly what the client yearns for. Develop your capacity for silence. Explore.

Often the client's assumptions get in their way. As coach, you will be challenging your client's assumptions on how life goes. You may be surfacing past conditioning of the client or simply their learned behaviors. These are opportunities to remind the client of their freedom of what to believe. It's their choice. When the content appears as therapeutic to you, it may be best to address it in the moment. For example, if a client mentions a past addiction and that they were in recovery, it's best to ask the questions in the moment to discover boundaries of the coaching relationship vs. coaching being a therapeutic activity. Will the client continue with their therapist as they work with a coach? Will the client bring up their addiction as an excuse in their coaching? Do they know where therapy ends and coaching begins? Setting clear expectations up front will provide a path of clarity for both coach and client.

One aspect to coaching that is similar to counseling is the dynamic of mirroring. As humans are social animals, there exists a yearning to be seen or witnessed as part of one's existence. You are that mirror. An aspect of coaching is to validate the client's expression of feelings and concerns. You are at the receiving end of their communication. They are paying you (either with time or money or both) to be their receiver. There may be times when your client wants a session to be a *download* of the week, and most of your time is spent there. After 20 minutes of download, for example, the client may be clear to then explore what's next in achieving their goal. But without that download you may have been coaching on top of stresses or concerns that would have derailed the coaching at one point or another.

Similar to listening, another core skill to coaching is asking questions. Your questions may reveal information needed for the maximum benefit to the client. Often, what we care deepest about doesn't get questioned. You as coach have an opportunity to assist the client in diving into what they most care about by the power of your questions. Your questions are to assist the client in discovering their path, and making their own best decisions. As both of you have the end state in mind, it takes an unbiased listener to ask the questions that uncover what's next for the client.

The structure of the coaching environment and how you come to the coaching session are key elements in the relationship. Are you upset by a past phone call? Do you have too many to-dos on your mind? The client will sense this, unless you get *cleared* to be present with the client. Often times conflict is started if the coach has internal conflicts. Therefore, it's best to use tools to become a *shiny reflective surface* for the client. Structuring the call or meeting to be 30, 45, 50, or 60 minutes will allow for both parties to plan and be ready for coaching. As the saying goes, "Good fences make good neighbors." Set boundaries for building trust and demonstrate your integrity to the session.

For some clients, you may be the sole source for supporting their goals — do you have the stamina and fortitude to hold their end state, even when the client may not? You will be tested. Your client will come up with excuses, statistics of why they can't, down feelings and up feelings. No matter how the client shows up, their desired end state is your compass. You also may be the only regular appointment for your client, especially if it is a weekly appointment. This consistent review of the client's goals is in itself a reinforcement to their commitment. Will you provide not only the structure, but also the continuous stand for their desires?

Some clients may ask you for advice or suggestions. This request sets up an *expert/non-expert* dynamic, which is not a coaching relationship. Your client is the expert on their life. If a client wants opinions or information, there are plenty of resources for them. Ask your client what would serve them best. If you happen to know something that may be of support, be sure to declare that your suggestion is outside of coaching so it tells the client you are outside the coaching relationship in the moment. Otherwise, they might assume coaching is something that it is not. For example, if you are also a communication trainer, you may say, "This isn't coaching. This comes from my communication training experience. It's said that 93% of communication is nonverbal, 7% words, 38% tonality, and 55% body language." And then jump back into your coaching hat: "What would you like to do with this information?"

People can be very interesting — and very entertaining. This can be a trap for coaches. This is not a session for the coach — it is a session for the client. If you find yourself interested or entertained, best to tell your client to see if it serves them. Do they know they have this affect? If so, is it serving them getting to their end state? Using direct communication about this with your client will build trust and the relationship.

Popular to coaching language is the term "off the court." For example, in basketball, if you are the coach, it's important that you are on the sidelines and not playing the game for the player. It is not enhancing the client's skills. The client could go home and watch some of the best basketball players of the world rather than watching their coach on the court. It would be a better use of their time. Let the client play their game of life. You are the coach. Be sure you are on the sidelines.

If your coaching relationship seems to be morphing into a friendship, it's another opportunity to use direct communication to retain the coaching framework. There are a number of ways to do this — simply being direct about what you notice, reminding the client of their desired end state and asking them how it's going, or reiterating what makes a coaching relationship and doing a check-in. Sometimes the best service to a client is to complete the coaching.

A friendship may follow the ending of a coaching relationship. It's best to have a conversation to ensure that the former client knows that you would not become a coach to that person again — formally or informally. A friendship within a coaching context is considered a dual relationship and does not serve the client nor your reputation as a coach. The focus is to remain on the client. Coaching friends clouds this dynamic and is best avoided. Referring friends to colleagues for coaching can be a nice referral system between you and other coaches.

One of the joys of being human is to self-discover and share one's story. Your role as coach may at times simply be to stand by as your clients bust through fears or blocks. You may elect to offer what is known as *spot coaching* between sessions. This is where you offer your time for 10 to 15 minutes on call (but not promising it will be right when they call you). This offer creates a greater sense of support as well as responsibility. If the client calls to let you know they have failed in some way, the call is an opportunity to create a new perspective around the failure. You may again provide choice, where without you, the client may feel victim to the failure. If your client starts abusing your spot coaching offer, let them know your boundaries.

A client may have an insight, but without an action to build upon that insight, it may remain just an idea and they run the risk of going back to old habits. Your role as a coach is to stimulate actions toward achieving that end state. Being in the moment with your client where you can capture insight — point to it and not let it slide — will serve the client. It becomes the moment of possibility for change. Clients seek change when they come to you. Your own comfort with change and innovation will be tested. Your concepts of what is possible will be pushed. How open are you to being a conduit for change?

CHAPTER 2

THE INTERNATIONAL COACH FEDERATION

A resource worth spending some time with is the International Coach Federation, also known as ICF. The Web site is www.coachfederation.org. In 1995, the ICF was founded to advance the coaching profession. There are now over 14,000 ICF member coaches in more than 90 countries. The purpose of ICF is to advance the art, science and practice of professional coaching. The ICF developed *The ICF Code of Ethics* and *The Ethical Conduct Review Process* for those who have ethical complaints against an ICF member. *The Code of Ethics* has two parts: "The Definition of Coaching," and "ICF Standards of Ethical Conduct" made up of Professional Conduct at Large, Conflicts of Interest, Professional Conduct with Clients, Confidentiality/Privacy, and the ICF Pledge of Ethics. If you are not yet an ICF member, it would serve you to include this kind of ethical pledge in some form.

Anyone can claim to be a coach, but when you have been credentialed by the ICF, it says you've been through a process with several steps, including many hours of experience as a coach and many hours receiving coaching from a mentor coach. Those who aren't members of the ICF and call themselves a coach may be misrepresenting coaching. Actual training or advice-giving or counseling may be taking place, which gives coaching a confusing identity.

The ICF can give your client a reference point to make sense out of this new industry. Since it is relatively new, it can be challenging to educate others to use a coach. Having a standard definition gives credit to the coaching profession.

There are currently 119 ICF accredited/approved coach training programs. All ICF approved/accredited programs can be found in the free Training Program Search Service at the ICF web site. At a minimum, becoming a member of the ICF adds credibility to your role as coach. You can become credentialed through an ICF application as well. It's up to you on which path to take to show your connection to the ICF.

ICF CORE COMPETENCIES

Coaching is self-regulated and as such, the ICF has created a globally recognized credential and code of ethics to assist consumers in selecting a coach. A coach who is credentialed by the ICF has completed stringent education and experience requirements and has demonstrated a strong commitment to excellence in coaching. Those who choose to become credentialed, are tested on their mastery of eleven core competencies developed by the ICF.

The following pages list these core competencies in detail. Please review them and be aware of your opinions of them. At the end of this chapter, I'd like you to rank them in order of importance to you.

Listed with permission from the ICF

SETTING THE FOUNDATION

I. Meeting Ethical Guidelines and Professional Standards

Understanding of coaching ethics and standards and ability to apply them appropriately in all coaching situations

1. Understands and exhibits in own behaviors the ICF Standards of Conduct (see www.coachingfederation.org: Part III of ICF Code of Ethics)

2. Understands and follows all ICF Ethical Guidelines (also on web site)

3. Clearly communicates the distinctions between coaching, consulting, psychotherapy and other support professions

4. Refers client to another support professional as needed, knowing when this is needed and the available resources

II. Establishing the Coaching Agreement

Ability to understand what is required in the specific coaching interaction and to come to agreement with the prospective and new client about the coaching process and relationship

1. Understands and effectively discusses with the client the guidelines and specific parameters of the coaching relationship (e.g., logistics, fees, scheduling, inclusion of others if appropriate)

2. Reaches agreement about what is appropriate in the

relationship and what is not, what is and is not being offered, and about the client's and coach's responsibilities

3. Determines whether there is an effective match between his/her coaching method and the needs of the prospective client

CO-CREATING THE RELATIONSHIP

III. Establishing Trust and Intimacy with the Client

Ability to create a safe, supportive environment that produces ongoing mutual respect and trust

1. Shows genuine concern for the client's welfare and future
2. Continuously demonstrates personal integrity, honesty and sincerity
3. Establishes clear agreements and keeps promises,
4. Demonstrates respect for client's perceptions, learning style, personal being
5. Provides ongoing support for and champions new behaviors and actions, including those involving risk taking and fear of failure
6. Asks permission to coach client in sensitive, new areas

IV. Coaching Presence

Ability to be fully conscious and create spontaneous relationship with the client, employing a style that is open, flexible and confident

1. Is present and flexible during the coaching process, dancing in the moment

2. Accesses own intuition and trusts one's inner knowing — "goes with the gut"

3. Is open to not knowing and takes risks

4. Sees many ways to work with the client and chooses in the moment what is most effective

5. Uses humor effectively to create lightness and energy

6. Confidently shifts perspectives and experiments with new possibilities for own action

7. Demonstrates confidence in working with strong emotions, and can self-manage and not be overpowered or enmeshed by client's emotions

COMMUNICATING EFFECTIVELY

V. Active Listening

Ability to focus completely on what the client is saying and is not saying, to understand the meaning of what is said in the context of the client's desires, and to support client self-expression

1. Attends to the client and the client's agenda and not to the coach's agenda for the client

2. Hears the client's concerns, goals, values and beliefs about what is and is not possible

3. Distinguishes between the words, the tone of voice, and the body language

4. Summarizes, paraphrases, reiterates, mirrors back what

client has said to ensure clarity and understanding

5. Encourages, accepts, explores and reinforces the client's expression of feelings, perceptions, concerns, beliefs, suggestions, etc.

6. Integrates and builds on client's ideas and suggestions

7. "Bottom-lines" or understands the essence of the client's communication and helps the client get there rather than engaging in long descriptive stories

8. Allows the client to vent or "clear" the situation without judgment or attachment in order to move on to next steps

VI. Powerful Questioning

Ability to ask questions that reveal the information needed for maximum benefit to the coaching relationship and the client

1. Asks questions that reflect active listening and an understanding of the client's perspective,

2. Asks questions that evoke discovery, insight, commitment or action (e.g., those that challenge the client's assumptions),

3. Asks open-ended questions that create greater clarity, possibility or new learning

4. Asks questions that move the client towards what they desire, not questions that ask for the client to justify or look backwards.

VII. Direct Communication

Ability to communicate effectively during coaching sessions and to use language that has the greatest positive impact on the client

1. Is clear, articulate and direct in sharing and providing feedback
2. Reframes and articulates to help the client understand from another perspective what he/she wants or is uncertain about
3. Clearly states coaching objectives, meeting agenda, purpose of techniques or exercises
4. Uses language appropriate and respectful to the client (e.g., non-sexist, non-racist, non-technical, non-jargon)
5. Uses metaphor and analogy to help to illustrate a point or paint a verbal picture

FACILITATING LEARNING AND RESULTS

VIII. Creating Awareness

Ability to integrate and accurately evaluate multiple sources of information and to make interpretations that help the client to gain awareness and thereby achieve agreed-upon results

1. Goes beyond what is said in assessing client's concerns, not getting hooked by the client's description
2. Invokes inquiry for greater understanding, awareness and clarity
3. Identifies for the client his/her underlying concerns, typical and fixed ways of perceiving himself/herself and

the world, differences between the facts and the interpretation, disparities between thoughts, feelings and action

4. Helps clients to discover for themselves the new thoughts, beliefs, perceptions, emotions, moods, etc. that strengthen their ability to take action and achieve what is important to them

5. Communicates broader perspectives to clients and inspires commitment to shift their viewpoints and find new possibilities for action

6. Helps clients to see the different, interrelated factors that affect them and their behaviors (e.g., thoughts, emotions, body, background)

7. Expresses insights to clients in ways that are useful and meaningful for the client

8. Identifies major strengths vs. major areas for learning and growth, and what is most important to address during coaching

9. Asks the client to distinguish between trivial and significant issues, situational vs. recurring behaviors, when detecting a separation between what is being stated and what is being done

IX. Designing Actions

Ability to create with the client opportunities for ongoing learning, during coaching and in work/life situations, and for taking new actions that will most effectively lead to agreed-upon coaching results

1. Brainstorms and assists the client to define actions that will enable the client to demonstrate, practice and deepen new learning

2. Helps the client to focus on and systematically explore specific concerns and opportunities that are central to agreed-upon coaching goals

3. Engages the client to explore alternative ideas and solutions, to evaluate options, and to make related decisions

4. Promotes active experimentation and self-discovery, where the client applies what has been discussed and learned during sessions immediately afterwards in his/her work or life setting

5. Celebrates client successes and capabilities for future growth

6. Challenges client's assumptions and perspectives to provoke new ideas and find new possibilities for action

7. Advocates or brings forward points of view that are aligned with client goals and, without attachment, engages the client to consider them

> pace of learning, to reflect on and learn from experiences)
>
> 10. Positively confronts the client with the fact that he/she did not take agreed-upon actions

All eleven competencies are important, but below you have an opportunity to give your personal opinion about each one. If you were to give each of the competencies a rating of importance on a scale of 1 to 10 (with 10 being the absolute "must-have" competency, and 1 being "not so important" competency), how would you rate them?

I. Meeting Ethical Guidelines and Professional Standards	_____
II. Establishing The Coaching Agreement	_____
III. Establishing Trust and Intimacy With The Client	_____
IV. Coaching Presence	_____
V. Active Listening	_____
VI. Powerful Questioning	_____
VII. Direct Communication	_____
VIII. Creating Awareness	_____
IX. Designing Actions	_____
X. Planning and Goal Setting	_____
XI. Managing Progress and Accountability	_____

Which of the competencies do you feel you are strongest in (choose at least one)?_____

_____

_____

Which of the competencies do you feel you are weakest in (choose at least one)?_____

_____

_____

Your answers will be revisited in later chapters.

CHAPTER **3**

INTRODUCTION TO THE STRENGTH DEPLOYMENT INVENTORY

Imagine you are at your desk in your office. You've recently accepted your new part-time role as a coach. At the moment, you are working on other aspects of your job when in walks Larry, an employee who you have taken on as your first coaching client. He asks if you have a minute and before you answer proceeds to sit in a chair to tell his story. "Now that we have this coaching relationship, I could really use your help. I've had it. This was the fifth time I've told Maria to include the data analysis in all outgoing proposals." His face looks tense and flushed. He continues, "You know what just happened? A prospect just called me to tell me we were weak in our data analysis and they've chosen another provider." You continue to listen to Larry and wonder if now is the best time for coaching. He says, "I need your help, I don't think I can talk to her. What do I do?"

There's more than one possible answer here, as there often is in coaching. Your gut reaction to this experience is that you'd do what you'd normally do speaking from what's important to you in the moment. Perhaps it's, "Larry, sorry I'm in the middle of something," or "Larry, I hear your frustration. I'd feel the same way. Let's grab a coffee". You are eager to be a coach to Larry, but are not sure if it's the right time. This is a new role and you've resorted to what you'd naturally do for a co-worker.

It is common that we assume we know how to communicate. After all, we've done it all our lives — how we construct sentences, our intonations, how we describe things, word choices, etc. We think it's understandable. Yet, the definition of "understandable" happens both from the sender and the receiver of communication. By looking at the *values* set underneath communication, we discover the meaning from which the person sees their communication as understandable.

As Victor Frankl states, "Man's search for meaning is the primary motivation in his life and not a 'secondary rationalization' of instinctual drives. This meaning is unique and specific in that it must and can be fulfilled by him alone; only then does it achieve a significance which will satisfy his own will to meaning. There are some authors who contend that meanings and values are 'nothing but defense mechanism, reaction formations and sublimations'. But as for myself, I would not be willing to live merely for the sake of my 'defense mechanisms,' nor would I be ready to die merely for the sake of my 'reaction formation.' Man, however is able to live and even to die for the sake of his ideals and values!" (Frankl, 1959)

A variety of values exist in the world, as well as a variety of ways to assess one's values. One could narrow down a list of hundreds of values to a select few or they could use an inventory that has reliability and validity measurements. The choice is yours on how you go about it.

Dr. Elias H. Porter developed a theory of human values (termed *Motivational Value System*) based on Erich Fromm's theory in <u>Man for Himself</u>. Porter's theory, called *Relationship Awareness Theory*,® involves an inventory (Strength Deployment Inventory® or SDI®) that measures one's values.

Relationship Awareness is founded on four simple, yet profound premises:

PREMISE 1: *Behavior is driven by motivation to achieve self-worth*
PREMISE 2: *Motivation changes in conflict*
PREMISE 3: *Strengths, when overdone or misapplied can be perceived as weaknesses*
PREMISE 4: *Personal filters influence perceptions of self and others*

To understand an application of these premises, take Larry as an example. Larry's behavior of walking right into your office is said to have a motivation behind it *(Premise 1)*.

Could it be he wants action now? Or that he needs harmony back in his day? Larry might be in conflict. Normally Larry is pretty laid back. Could this be a sign that he is in conflict because he doesn't seem so laid back in the moment? *(Premise 2)*

Larry has interrupted your day. Now he might see this as a needed behavior. He has heard that his coach would help him in a pinch.

Well this is his *pinch*. So what he sees as a strength to come to you right away with an issue, may come off as a weakness for you as it seemed uncaring and rash. ***(Premise 3)***

You realize you would never go into another person's office and begin speaking before getting acknowledgment that they were available. Noticing how you do things can show you your filter on your perception, which may be how rude it was of him to not wait for an acknowledgment. ***(Premise 4)***

Relationship Awareness Theory, like many psychological theories, holds that all people want to have relationships with other people. From birth, humans seek positive connections with their care-givers. It is through interactions and relationships with others that we exist and that our world has meaning. Therefore, our behaviors are expressions of this desire to be connected with others. Relationship Awareness Theory looks at how we go about establishing and maintaining these relationships in order to have a positive sense of ourselves and our value as a person.

Relationship Awareness Theory is a *motivational theory*, which addresses the motives or purposes that are behind everyday behavior when we are relating to others. It assumes that there is meaning behind all behavior. By shifting our focus from only looking at behavior to looking at the purpose behind the behavior, we can gain a clearer understanding of ourselves and others.

In Relationship Awareness Theory, behavior is looked at in the following way:

- Behaviors are tools used to get some result or confirm our sense of self-worth.
- Motives come from our wish to feel a strong sense of self-worth or self-value.
- Our individual Motivational Value System is consistent throughout our life and underpins all of our behaviors.
- Traditional writing about motivation describes motives as something that can be inspired in others. Here, motives are thought of as already present in every person and readily available to be tapped.

In Relationship Awareness Theory, motives are a basic antecedent of behavior. In other words, motives in this theory are the "why" we do what we do.

Relationship Awareness Theory identifies seven general themes or clusters of motives. In looking at these clusters, we notice that certain behaviors are associated with each cluster. The behaviors, however, are not unique to any particular cluster. For example, one of the clusters has to do with a desire to be altruistic and nurturing. People who are motivated by this desire tend to exhibit behaviors that are seen by others as being helpful. Helpful behavior, though, can be exhibited by people who have other motive clusters. The difference is one of frequency. People who are motivated by a desire to be altruistic and nurturing are likely to behave more frequently in ways that are intended to be helpful to others than people who have other motive clusters. There is also more consistency over time in exhibiting helpful behaviors by those who are motivated by a desire to be altruistic and nurturing.

These clusters are called Motivational Value Systems (MVS). There are seven identifiable styles of relating to others when things are going well for an individual:

- Altruistic–Nurturing (Blue)
- Assertive–Directing (Red)
- Analytic–Autonomizing (Green)
- Flexible–Cohering (Hub)
- Assertive–Nurturing (Red-Blue Blend)
- Judicious–Competing (Red-Green Blend)
- Cautious–Supporting (Blue-Green Blend)

See Appendix A for descriptions of each MVS.

Dr. Porter developed the Strength Deployment Inventory to help people access, understand, and use Relationship Awareness Theory. When you complete the inventory you, learn about your values that underlie your behaviors in two types of conditions: when all is going well, and when things are in conflict. With this knowledge, you will better understand yourself and your clients.

Now that you have an overview of Relationship Awareness Theory, you are encouraged to complete a SDI (Strength Deployment Inventory) of your own. Go to the following web link: www.personalstrengths.us/sdiincoachingoffer and enter coupon code 381210 for a discount.

CHAPTER **4**

KNOW THYSELF

Remember Larry from the previous chapter? He is still sitting in your office. You think to yourself, "How would I want to be responded to if I had this issue?" You think you'd want to discuss your feelings, so you proceed to ask Larry, "I hear what happened, how is this making you feel?" Larry has a quizzical look on his face and says, "How I feel is immaterial. I want action. I want this fixed. I can't stand losing a client." You realize that your question may not have been what this client really needed. You would have liked a response like you gave, but Larry looks more irritated.

If you were working with a coach, wouldn't you want them to tell you if any of their comments or questions were *rose-colored*? Influence can happen subtly. As a coach, you'll want to *stay off the court* from your clients. Knowing your values helps you to realize your bias and allows the client to play their game.

Identifying your values as a coach also helps to identify those of your client. It gives you a view of the palette of values available to your own client's painting of the world. Without this, you may be swayed by your values unconsciously and wonder why your client does not respond, or even why they have ended the coaching relationship. For example, if you value trust and connection over the other values, your coaching may be swayed in this area. The client may need more focus on being accountable and creating results. In addition, certain values may have you excel at some competencies and not others *(more on this in the next chapter)*.

The Strength Deployment Inventory not only addresses your values when things are going well, but also how your values shift when you are in conflict. This is helpful if you feel yourself shift during your coaching session. Also, your client may be in conflict with you and it is helpful to know how to identify this shift. Chapter 7 will look more closely at the subject of conflict.

If you haven't yet had your SDI debrief by visiting the following page: www.personalstrengths.us/sdiincoaching, please refer to the SDI Interpretive Guide in Appendix A. There you will find brief descriptions of the 7 Motivational Value Systems, how motivation may change in conflict, and how each of the value sets may "overdo" their strengths.

Now that you know your own set of values, how does this affect your coaching? Here are a few examples:

BLUE (Altruistic-Nurturing): Tend to focus more on the client's feelings and how their actions may impact others... May show more support and appreciation of the client... May avoid being direct, thinking it will do more harm than good.

RED (Assertive–Directing): Tend to focus more on the actions the client is or isn't doing... May miss moments of insight from the client that are coming across as clear and direct... May challenge the client too frequently or with too much force.

GREEN (Analytic–Autonomizing): Tend to focus more on the information relayed from the client... May miss subtle changes in emotion or intonation... May lack empathy or not show empathy.

RED-BLUE (Assertive–Nurturing): Tend to focus on actions they think are good for the client, rather than co-creating the actions... May not gather the information from the client as easily as *going by their gut*.

RED-GREEN (Judicious–Competing): Tend to envision the next steps with the client and push for what they see based on the relayed facts from the client... May spend more time *figuring out* the client than coaching.

BLUE-GREEN (Cautious–Supporting): Tend to focus on giving the client enough space to be self-sufficient... May miss moments to be direct and challenge assumptions... May be too quiet intending to be respectful of the client's process and lose the client's engagement.

HUB (Flexible–Cohering): Tend to be more social, and playful which may be distracting... Tends to tell tangential stories... May be more flexible than is needed.

Please review the preceding list and think about your own possible self-limiting tendencies when it comes to coaching. Write what you notice below:

_____

_____

_____

_____

_____

_____

_____

_____

Knowing that your tendencies are based on your values, you can now self-correct as you coach.

You can intentionally choose what to do the moment you sense your bias surfacing. Examples may include: creating a break in the call, being transparent and sharing the bias, discontinuing the bias and continuing coaching, apologizing for the bias at the end of the call and seeing what there is to "clean up."

Staying unbiased can be likened to a judge who must remain impartial until information shared shows the next steps. Your client is the one who comes with a solution — they are asking for a coach to help them see it. Knowing your values bias will help you in allowing the client's process to emerge.

Without seeing your bias, you'll be 'being' your bias.

Your role as coach is not to *force-fit* your clients into your value system. However, you don't need to forfeit your value system. After all, your value system may be the reason you became a coach in the first place. For which values did you become a coach?

Here are some possible reasons:

BLUE: To support and help others

RED: To accept the challenges of coaching others to get results

GREEN: To validate my own belief in the process of coaching with a methodical approach

RED-BLUE: To show I care for others through my actions

RED-GREEN: To enter a new market/challenge with a thoughtful approach

BLUE-GREEN: To help others by instilling a coaching process where they become self-sufficient in reaching their goals

HUB: To exercise flexibility and work with a variety of clients

Write your thoughts on which of your values you support by being a coach below:

_____

_____

_____

_____

_____

_____

The reasons why you became a coach are helpful to your professional description of your coaching intent or your professional mission in coaching. It can have a negative impact if it interferes with the client's agenda during your coaching. Some warning signs when it does: clients become irritated more often, clients become quiet more often, you notice a shift in the rapport with your client, and yes, some clients will discontinue the coaching relationship. Some clients may stay, but not receive the breakthroughs that propel them to their goals because the coaching is focused on your values and not so much on theirs. Without seeing your bias, you'll be *being* your bias.

CHAPTER 5

EACH COMPETENCY EXPLORED

So now Larry is more irritated (as noted in the previous chapter). You've started to realize that what you thought would be helpful to Larry really was what would be helpful if *you* were in a similar situation. Talking about your feelings and how to bring harmony to the situation, you realize you came from your value system of Blue in the SDI. You're going to take an educated guess that Larry has a Red motivation, so you clean up your biased rookie move, and say, "Larry, I appreciate you letting me know your feelings don't matter in this moment. As we work more together, I'll expect this kind of feedback so we can stay on track. Just so I'm clear, what do you want as an ideal outcome? And please put it in terms of something that is specific, measurable, achievable and a result in time." Larry pauses and with some enthusiasm says, "I want all proposals starting today to go out with the data analysis." You realize you are back in rapport with Larry, and it's good to know what your values are so you can watch for them interrupting your coaching success.

Your Motivational Value System may draw your attention and priority to certain ICF competencies, potentially even creating a bias. Because your MVS is part of the way you create meaning for yourself, you may subconsciously choose to focus on competencies that more closely align with your personal values. This means you may also be neglecting some of the other coaching competencies if they don't align as closely with your personal values. The good news is, you get to become aware of your natural pull and be more conscious in your choices.

Taking a look at each of the competencies below, note where you may be naturally inclined to put your energy. Place a check mark next to the items you think are your natural strengths. The description below each competency is modified from the ICF description to suggest common values concerns of that competency to the Motivational Value Systems of the SDI.

_____ 1. MEETING ETHICAL GUIDELINES
AND PROFESSIONAL STANDARDS
Demonstrates concern for assurance that things have been properly thought out; uses cautious, thorough, fair, decision-making with authentic criteria; understands coaching ethics and standards of conduct; communicates distinctions between coaching, consulting and other support professions (Green MVS)

_____ 2. ESTABLISHING THE COACHING AGREEMENT
Able to understand what is required in the coaching interaction; discusses the guidelines, parameters of the relationship, structure of coaching, what it is, what it isn't, responsibilities of coach and of client; matches methods with needs (Blue-Green MVS)

_____ 3. ESTABLISHING TRUST AND
INTIMACY WITH THE CLIENT

Shows genuine concern for client; demonstrates sincerity; creates safe, supportive environment with ongoing support; asks permission to coach client in sensitive new areas (Blue MVS)

_____ 4. COACHING PRESENCE

Creates spontaneous relationship; is open to not knowing; experiments with new possibilities for own action; demonstrates an open and flexible style; uses humor; is playful, dancing in the moment; sees many ways of working with clients (Hub MVS)

_____ 5. ACTIVE LISTENING

Supports client in self-expression; attends to client's agenda; hears the client; distinguishes between words, tones, body language, and encourages expression of feelings; builds on clients' ideas and suggestions; allows client to vent or *clear* the situation (Red-Blue MVS)

_____ 6. POWERFUL QUESTIONING

Asks questions that reveal the information needed for maximum benefit to the coaching relationship and the client; asks questions that reflect an understanding of the client's perspective; asks questions that evoke discovery; asks open-ended questions that create greater clarity or new learning; asks questions that move the client towards what the client desires (Green MVS)

_____ 7. DIRECT COMMUNICATION

Is clear, articulate, and direct in giving feedback; reframes and clearly states objectives, agenda and purpose (Red MVS)

_____ 8. CREATING AWARENESS

Integrates multiple sources of information; notices differences and disparities in the client's speaking; helps clients identify actions and what is important to them; communicates broader perspectives; helps them see different interrelated factors (Hub MVS)

_____ 9. DESIGNING ACTIONS

Creates with the client, taking new actions that lead to agreed-upon results; brainstorms defining actions and focus; challenges client's assumptions; engages the client to explore ideas; promotes active experimentation and self-discovery and applies it immediately in real life settings, "do it now" (Red-Blue MVS)

_____ 10. PLANNING AND GOAL SETTING

Maintains effective coaching plan; consolidates collected information; helps client identify resources for learning; creates a plan with results that are attainable, measurable, specific, and have target dates; identifies early successes (Red-Green MVS)

_____ 11. MANAGING PROGRESS AND ACCOUNTABILITY

Clearly requests actions to move client toward goal; demonstrates follow-through; acknowledges client for what they've done and haven't done; holds client accountable; positively confronts clients when s/he did not take agree upon actions; effectively prepares client information obtained during the sessions; able to move back and forth between big picture of where client is heading, what is discussed, and where client wishes to go (Hub MVS)

Now that you can see the Motivational Value Systems associated with each competency, look back at your ratings at the end of Chapter 2. Can you see why you may have rated them the way you did?

Did you select the most important competencies based on your MVS?

Did you select your strongest competencies that match your MVS?

Did you select your weakest as those outside your MVS?

How does this validate your bias coming from your MVS?

_____

_____

_____

_____

_____

What action plan will you create based on your answers above? *Example: I realize I am focusing on my need for my clients to be methodical and data-driven (because of my Green MVS) and perhaps not creating a supportive environment. I want to practice Establishing Trust and Intimacy With The Client.*

_____

_____

_____

_____

_____

_____

CHAPTER **6**

CREATING MEANING
FOR YOUR CLIENT

You are feeling better about the rapport with Larry and have made an educated guess that his Motivational Value System is Red, but how can you be sure? You could ask for his SDI result, but instead you ask a different question, "Larry, it's important to me as your coach to support you in realizing your goals and I don't want to assume I know why it's important for you to reach those goals. So that I can provide you with customized coaching, let me ask you a question. This may seem like an obvious answer, but sometimes I may not see things the same way as a client. If you achieved your goal (of having all proposals going out with the data analysis) within the next two hours, why is that meaningful for you?"

Larry replies, "I'm not like other consultants here. I don't think acting quickly to get out a proposal means anything. I've done the research to prove the best pathway. I want it included even if it takes an extra hour to type it in. I really dislike stupid acts. There's no reason for them. It's meaningful for me to have the prospective client see me as not only responsive, but as a smart and responsive consultant."

You thank Larry for his clarification. This detailed response has helped you see he is more on the side of Red-Green in the SDI. So you suggest, "Thank you, Larry that was helpful. I'd like to suggest that we have a plan to support you not only in the goals that are written in your performance development plan, but also a plan for getting this action accomplished today."

Larry replies, "Now that's something I can get into."

It's not only what you communicate, but how you communicate that can create a successful interaction. When you relate better to your client's values, and focus on the ICF core competencies, your coaching potential is unlimited.

So what will help you get there? First thing is to recognize when you are overdoing your most common behaviors. Please refer to the Managing Your Strengths list in Appendix A. Let's take, for example, the behavior of being Analytical. When overdone, this behavior can be experienced as Nit picking. Or take the behavior of Helpful. When overdone, this can be experienced as smothering. Your client may not appreciate a coach who is nit picking or smothering. A behavior may not seem to be overdone to you, but what matters here is how the client is experiencing your behavior.

Having a reminder system near you when coaching can support you in your awareness of your behaviors. Using a technique such as notes posted to your computer or wall reminding you of your top behaviors will assist your awareness. You can also begin to get feedback from others. For example, hand a list of strengths or overdone strengths to your client, friend, or family member and ask them what they think you tend to overdo.

When you experience a *rapport* with your client, you are matching well to what is needed in the moment. When you notice unusual silences, or voiced discomfort, you may have hit an area for exploration, or you may have just overdone a behavior. Check in with the client. Examples of checking in include, "Would you like me to say this in a different way?", or simply, "What's going on for you in this moment?"

If you are interested in expanding your client base, whether as an external or internal coach, consider how you market your service both verbally and written. Do you notice a values bias in these forms of marketing? If so, you are most likely attracting clients that match your values. Therefore you may be leaving 6/7th (remember there are 7 Motivational Value Systems in total) of prospective clients untapped. Develop your language to reach all values, and you develop your potential for more clients.

When you meet a person for the first time, and learn about his or her desired end state, you have the opportunity to inquire, "And what will that give you?" This is an opportunity to learn about the values behind the end state. If you did not receive enough of an answer, a follow-up question may be used, such as, "What part of you will you be most proud of when you reach that end state?"

With noticing your client's values, you then can proceed to use language that will truly mean something for the client. You, the coach, have choice in how you deliver your communication. Choose wisely. Through this choice you have the potential to prevent conflict with your client and enhance their sense of identity and self-worth.

It may be helpful to think of the analogy of learning a new foreign language. If your client understood Spanish as their main language, wouldn't you want to use what they understand, versus what you are most comfortable with? Speaking your client's language will add power and velocity to your coaching.

Feel free to use your own values as examples for your client. If you know you have Red as your Motivational Value System, let your client know you tend to focus there. The client will appreciate your candor and learn why you come across the way you do. This will help to build trust in the relationship. As you experience it in the moment, you could say, "I know I'm on a tangent right now and tend to go on tangents. I promise I will be connecting this to your point in just a moment" This may look like an overdone Hub or Blue strength to a person who has a Red or Green Motivational Value System.

In turn, when you begin to reflect your client's values in statements, such as, "I can appreciate you want a methodical approach to your goal. How would you go about it?" (Green values) Without necessarily taking an inventory, such as the Strength Deployment Inventory, your client can learn about their values through your noticing of them. He or she can learn what they tend to "overdo" with your simple reflection of it in the moment.

Sometimes, using the language of your client may not create rapport. There are many possible reasons for this. One reason is an advanced concept within Relationship Awareness Theory termed *masking*. Masking is a conditioned way of thinking and acting in the world that is used to survive a situation. For example, a person who had to grow up in a challenging environment of many siblings and absent parents, may have had to mask Red behavior to get what they wanted from their relationships. Later in life, this way of being still exists, but it is not meaningful for them because it is based in surviving. You as the coach have an opportunity to support this person through their growth to find what is truly meaningful for them. You may want to inquire what is meaningful versus what is *acceptable*, *practical*, or *assumed*. Don't worry if you don't break through a mask. This person has been wearing it for a lifetime. Even if the mask stays on, the client can receive value from coaching. This is why the ICF core competencies, in addition to values, are an effective combination.

As a reminder, it's not up to you to determine what your client's path is. Think of yourself as a Sherpa along the way, supplying what is requested by your client. You are walking the path together — not leading, or following. Pushing for your will is not a coaching technique. There's a time for direct, clear communication, but it will be used in support of your client's goal achievement, not for what *you* want. It is the client's insight, paired with co-designed actions, that lead to success. See Appendix B for a Client Preparation Sheet to guide you.

CHAPTER 7

BLOCKS HAPPEN

O ften in the client's request for coaching is a desire to see and to remove obstacles. You play a pivotal role. You will be asked to speak to those obstacles — to poke at places of fear and insecurities, all in the service of the client. In the previous chapters, the focus was on the coach not adding conflict into the relationship. By knowing your values and those of the client, you can create more of the atmosphere of trust and comfort. By your coaching presence, active listening, powerful questioning and direct communication, the relationship is strengthened.

What if the client is in conflict? Perhaps with themselves or a co-worker or loved one? How can you continue to coach? First off, your accepting of the client right where they are, in the conflict, may be something they have never experienced before — a listener who does not judge, run away, blame, or try to fix it. This alone can be powerful. Your accepting presence creates the space for continued sharing and trust building. Remember, the client contracted with you to get to an end state and now something is in their way. Often that something is a block or conflict. They want your coaching to create change.

Some blocks will be obvious to you. Client's may use words like, "that's impossible," "that's unreasonable," "that's ridiculous," "I can't," "I shouldn't," or "I won't succeed." Some blocks are disguised and may take a few sessions to surface. Building on the competency of creating trust supports the client to share what is in the way. Some blocks may be political in nature. If you coach internally in an organization, you may have very high trust-building skills, yet your role in the organization may give another signal to the client that they can not be at full disclosure. If you sense this in your sessions, directly communicating with the client about the business relationship is important. If you cannot come to an agreement suitable to the client's goals, offering an external coach may be the best option.

Blocks are common. Remember riding a bike or skating on ice for the first time? The biggest block may have been, "I don't want to fall!" But the vision of what it could be like once on that bike or skating on that ice is so compelling that you were willing to risk. People are often afraid of making things worse, so they keep progress at bay for some illusion of control of their current safety. One's conditioning and past experiences can have a big impact. You'll hear, "The last time I did something like this, I... lost my job, lost face, looked stupid." You might offer your client the juxtaposition of standing on the side of the ice rink or watching others enjoy their bike ride. Is their vision compelling enough to move forward?

Blocks are often stimulated by circumstances in the client's life — the boss won't sign off on their idea or a budget being cut. A block may appear where the client (in their mind) has made you into a teacher, boss, or parent and therefore behaves in ways that look good. Although these blocks appear to be on the outside, your role is to assist the client in seeing what part they play in their belief about the circumstance.

Take, for example, a client I worked with who was a manager. He felt put down by his boss in every encounter. After coaching this manager on what part he played in this regular ritual, he learned he hadn't been speaking directly and powerfully. Rather he tried to "play nice." Once he realized this, he asked to practice with me on speaking clearly and making powerful requests. This new behavior at work not only gave him more confidence with his boss, but subsequently had him promoted to a more senior project.

Another client, an entrepreneur, chose a profession that was not getting her the income to do the things she really wanted to do. Her focus in life was on finding out why this was happening. During coaching, she realized this conflict was giving her a boring life and not the life of her dreams. She also saw how she was holding this one aspect of life as the key to opening up all the others. "If only this profession created the money to explore these other areas," she thought. She decided to begin living the life of her dreams in small steps — doing research at night, meeting people who had the same interests — and soon she was living into her dreams and consequently her business began to flourish.

Another client was placing blame on a friend for not *acting like a friend*. When she realized her part in this circumstance and how her behaviors affected the result, she chose a new way of relating. She began to listen better to her friend and state what she wanted from the friendship. She created her friend by acting like a friend.

How do you recognize a block? One indicator is that clients may shift their behaviors when talking about an issue. There are those who would rather think about their conflict, gather more data, talk about how this issue occurred, and then process it. Others may be demonstrative and directive in their speech. Or some will say they hope it just works out and that the relationship is more important than a resolution. The Strength Deployment Inventory (SDI) may be of benefit here as it assesses how one responds to conflict. If used early on in the coaching relationship, the coach and client can agree that the coach has permission to address the shift he notices in the client. If you don't use the SDI, alternatively you can ask your client at the beginning of the relationship, "We may hit upon uncomfortable places for you. What should I look for when you are in conflict? How might you change your behavior? May I have permission to bring this up with you?" Let them know you intend to support them through blocks in support of their goals.

Addressing the conflict directly with powerful questions can create awareness for your client that shifts not only how they see things in their current situation, but also how they see things in life. For instance, remind them of their goal, and ask, "How does your perception of this conflict limit you from getting what you want?" Once clients begin to realize their perception is a powerful thing, they often have an "aha" moment, and are grateful for sharing the conflict — sometimes even grateful for having the conflict. Some may stay stuck in the process awhile longer and simply are relieved to voice it. Hearing comments such as, "Well it's out now," "That feels better," or "Now that I see it, what's next?" are indicators of the client processing their conflict. You may offer to summarize their comment and inquire back, "What's next?" This can support them in creating a new possibility to achieving what they want.

If the client is resistant to looking at their conflict and chooses to be the victim of their circumstance, this reflection back to them is often helpful. Some clients may be uncoachable on the topic. Once a client was so resistant to looking on her side of the fence that I asked, "Are you coachable on this topic?" She answered, "I guess not." After the session, I wondered if I had failed her somehow. At the next session she told me she thought a lot about being uncoachable and realized her goals were too important not to be coachable and therefore opened up to the topic once again.

Much of coaching is to remind the client of their potential and possibility to create change — that they can be *responsible* for how things go vs. the *victim* of how things go. Circumstances happen, and rather than our reaction, it's our response that creates leadership and self-care.

Identification of the conflict by the client is the gateway to learning. Creating awareness followed by an action is key to moving the client forward. Often the action is an assignment between sessions, but sometimes it may occur during the session. I've had clients call their colleague or family member on the phone during a session to request what they truly want or to heal a damaged relationship. There are times that the conflict may be too raw, so in creating the action you may sense that the client's readiness or energy level is low. An action for the week may simply be to take extra good care of themselves or journal about the topic. The client will let you know what they can take on as you co-create their assignments. A client was so impacted by her insight she told me she wanted the week to just let it sink in and she promised to come back with an action. A self-aware client will make such requests. If it becomes a pattern, inquire if their pattern supports their goal.

While coaching, you may experience the same conflict more than once in your client. That's one reason your listening of the client is so important. Bringing attention to the pattern arising again creates awareness for the client. They then can choose what to do with that insight – continue the pattern or change. Asking the client to take a 30,000-foot view on their context (way of thinking) invites the client to recognize their own patterns.

Sometimes you may sense a client is being defensive, yet their words are *textbook perfect client* stating what they know is possible and that they will change. Your role is also to notice the tone and underlying attitude of the client. Asking about what you sense can create a deeper awareness. Asking powerfully how this way of being may add to their conflict is good grounds for exploration.

It's common, especially when a person first starts their role as coach, that they feel responsible if the client doesn't get their block resolved in that same session. Here it is good to remember the process of coaching and the ICF competencies. Creating awareness may come in steps, rather than the big "aha" moment. Coaches' egos can get in the way of truly extraordinary work. If you don't have a coach, I highly recommend working with one to strengthen your own skills and build the capacity to stay *off the court.*

Assisting your client through conflict can have exponential results. Spending coaching time on the conflict can assist in identifying what is truly valued and meaningful for them. I have had clients work through conflicts and realize how they held themselves back. Once they saw this they could create their future actions, but we needed to go into the conflicts first. This occurs in the willingness to accept and honor their conflict and assisting them in making powerful choices.

The client is ultimately responsible for how they choose to behave and how they see things. You could avoid their pain and hope it works out, but you wouldn't be a coach. You'd be just another person in their life. You've been chosen as a coach to support movement to greater success. Spend the time with your client in the conflict, look at it with them, ask questions and assist in their awareness. Conflict can be just the thing that draws their attention to the costs of their current behavior, prompts them to make a new choice and take action that moves them closer to their goal.

CHAPTER **8**

PUTTING IT ALL TOGETHER: STORIES OF COACHING TO CLIENTS' VALUES

To incorporate one's knowledge of the ICF core competencies with the knowledge of human values, is to integrate a coaching methodology with a relationship methodology. These are two powerful means to supporting a client. The scenarios that follow provide a looking glass view of what is possible when one uses both tools in the coaching context. Similar to the snowflake, no one coaching interaction resembles that of another. Each is unique and non-repeatable.

(The names of the clients are protected for confidentiality purposes.)

Client: Grant

When I first met Grant, he stressed it was important to him to have at least two meetings before coming to a decision on who the best-fit coach would be. We had two meetings over two months before he said, "Yes, from what you've provided, I've chosen to work with you." In *Setting the Foundation*, he was highly receptive to learning the differences between coaching and therapy, and said that he appreciated the background knowledge to these two modalities. He asked more questions than the average client. He also appreciated the thought that the coach and the client are on an *equal footing*, and that there was not a hierarchy, but rather a type of "fairness" in his words.

I began to notice the Green (Analytical Autonomizing) Motivational Value System and chose to add more explanation and introduction to concepts and questions I had of Grant. It was important for him to know the background before answering a question. This, in turn, would build a sense of trust between us. Green, in particular, responds to a history of information before presenting the current state. My *Coaching Presence* was more patient, such as giving adequate time for pauses and processing of the words. In my *Active Listening*, I used more Green value-based words to preface my listening, such as, "If I understand you correctly…" or, "If this is right for you, what's next?" *Powerful questions* at times would create awareness of Grant's belief system. I recall asking him, "What do you notice about your thinking right in this moment?" "Does this way of right and wrong thinking serve you in regards to your goals?" and "How might it be limiting you?"

Although coaches reflect the language that connects to the clients' values, there may be times when we challenge the use of certain values for certain situations. For example, imagine that the goal of the client is to increase their ability to network with others. The Green values of fair and cautious may come off as cold and uncaring to others. The coach can be the one to point this out and ask the client to choose how they want to be in the networking interaction.

Direct Communication with Grant often took a fact-based approach. It often looked like this: "In our last conversation you said you wanted to go to three networking meetings this week and you went to one. What do you see?" *Creating Awareness* with Grant was often through questioning of his patterns. For example, "I've noticed that your action items from the past three weeks aren't being met and you mention how busy your week has been. How would you characterize your relationship to your action items?" For *Designing Actions,* he held actions as very important and was methodical in his approach. Sometimes Grant wrote his goals very accurately and specifically, stating that he would finish the goal by a particular hour on a certain day. Yet they were not being accomplished. He realized that his strength was creating plans, but that he was weak at completing them. He chose to re-set his goals so that when I had been focused on *Managing Progress and Accountability,* he could build the skills of not only goal planning, but take his completion rate more seriously. He then practiced a slightly higher bar vs. something that was deflating his power. Grant re-set his goals by not setting them so high, but still at a level that would challenge him. He realized he needed to make incremental goals to get to his ideal. In addition, when Grant completed his coaching time with me, he had re-designed his current position by borrowing Red behaviors with his boss — most notably in self-confidence and clear, direct communication.

Client: Beth

Beth came to me from a referral. She supported herself by working two jobs: one to give advice to those in a disenfranchised population and the other in sales to help people find their dream home. What I first noticed about Beth was how genuinely appreciative she was of the coaching interaction. She shared her excitement and gratitude for the relationship in almost every call. Through my own filter, I had a moment or two of thinking, "This is overdone blue," yet I knew that it was my hub-filter creating the thought. I mirrored back my appreciation of her being there and continued to *Set the Foundation* by mentioning that our relationship is supported by the ICF Code of Ethics and my promise of confidentiality. In *Establishing the Coaching Agreement*, I heightened the emphasis on our interaction being on an even basis — not one up or one down, but rather like two people rowing a boat. We both would need to paddle fairly equally to keep the coaching relationship boat moving forward. For example, in each session I would ask her what her request for coaching would be for that session. Her part of rowing would be to have a request.

I remember a distinct moment of conflict as her voice slowed down and she said, "I'll have to think about that." The issue was related to a physical ailment she had had for quite some time. With the intention of *Establishing Trust*, as well as upholding ethics, I asked how this ailment might affect her success in coaching. This is where she turned quiet — a possible indication of internal conflict. Upon experiencing her shift, I recalled my words and gathered she may have taken my question negatively. So I inquired about it, "I just noticed a change in your voice. What happened just then?" She continued to be quiet. I chose to be more vulnerable noticing that perhaps the trust was not yet fully established.

I continued, "Beth, when I asked the question of your ailment impacting your success in coaching, I did not intend for it to come off as judgment. I apologize if that's how it sounded. For us to work closer and for you to get the results you desire, I'm curious how you place this ailment in our coaching relationship and how you would like my support?" Beth began to speak, explaining that she was receiving psychological counseling for the issue. I asked if I might share some information on how the differences of counseling and coaching would support her and she agreed. After this sharing, her voice gained more speed and returned back to her regular cadence — she had made it back to feeling good about herself. I reflected this change back to her in *Active Listening* and asked what insight she had gained from it. She realized she did switch into a different attitude and perhaps a defense. With *Creating Awareness*, we co-created some actions for the next time she feels this shift in attitude; she would practice continuing to speak to the other person and let them know she would need to think about the topic and get back to them. It was an insightful learning for Beth which she then used to create her future and success in communications.

I asked Beth if we could come to an agreement regarding how her ailment would interface with coaching, "What would you like its impact to be?" She said, "No impact at all. I don't want it to interfere." I requested that during our coaching she not use the physical ailment as a reason for failure and if it did come up that way, I'd have permission to bring her attention to it. (*Powerful Questioning and Direct Communication*)

She agreed and thanked me for the care I showed for the sensitivity to her feelings. We had successfully managed our way through her first conflict.

Her goals focused on getting better results for the populations she served, not that they weren't satisfied, but that she wasn't satisfied with her monetary results. She simply wanted to learn how to work smarter and not harder. During continued coaching she realized she was uncomfortable creating structures to create these results (*Creating Awareness*). She realized she had always assumed just getting to be with people would create the results she wanted. She offered to practice using structures and was excited to have accountability to her coach to try something new and uncomfortable for her. She said she was great at supporting others, but that supporting herself for results wasn't familiar. It came to be that the competencies that seem more Red and Green would add so much more to her life (*Designing Actions, Planning and Goal Setting,* and *Managing Progress and Accountability*). The up-front trust-building and honoring her Blue while coaching, assisted her in trusting that the Red-Green aspects could work in her life. At the end of each call, she voiced her appreciation saying that they were challenging assignments, but she knew I was there to support her in trying new things.

Client: Rose

I clearly remember my first conversation with Rose. She said, "I don't want any feel-good-fluffy-stuff, I want someone to keep me to my commitments and hold me accountable to results." My response was to jump right to *Direct Communication*, "I can be that for you. I can't promise I won't go to any feel-good-fluffy-stuff, but I will ask that you let me know when you hear it." She agreed. Trust was established, this time in a direct way. I could feel myself slightly challenged by her motivation, but also interested in practicing to deliver my coaching using more Red language.

I introduced *Establishes the Foundation & Coaching Agreement*, in this way, "The following information may seem tedious to get through, but the intention behind it is to provide you a clear platform in which you can achieve results. To use an analogy, if you were a trapeze artist wanting to create the result of a triple somersault in the air, you'd want a net or trampoline under you. These principles serve as the trampoline to bounce you back on the bars." She responded, "Okay, what d'ya got?" Trust was again established by telling her this isn't going to come off direct and to bear with me. She stayed engaged.

Coaching Presence was the unique challenge for me as my energy needed to mirror hers and she had aspirations she wanted to create quickly. I often paraphrased her stories of work situations into short phrases, which became a mechanism for her insight. She was often frustrated by the content of her stories. Hearing them paraphrased to get to the essence of her conflict assisted her learning. For example, she often volunteered for work assignments and was disappointed she wasn't getting recognition for her efforts. She was creating a no-win situation for herself. She continued to volunteer thinking it was amounting to some recognition, but never discussing with her boss if her volunteer time was valuable for the organization.

Sometimes the client can move faster than you think. I often find clients with a Red motivation to be willing to take risks — an asset to their coaching experience. Rose's conflict was that she wanted recognition from others, but never asked for it. She then created tasks that brought her face-to-face with her supervisor to get feedback. She started to learn what was really rewarded vs. what she thought should be "obviously" rewarded.

After two months of coaching and fulfilling her action plans, she realized the organization wasn't the ideal environment for her and the culture of the organization was not a good fit. We made a plan for transition while she completed another goal of creating a film script. After she had the transition plan set, she ended coaching. She promised to email me when the script was done and let me know how her transition was going. Within two months she did exactly what she said she was going to do and was pleased with the outcome. She had finished the script, was working freelance for her old company, and had begun searching for a fulfilling work environment. It was fascinating to notice my own hub filter that she got what she wanted without a lot of focus on emotions. It was a wonderful reminder that clients have their own definition and celebration of success.

Client: Helen

Helen, a senior hospital administrator, came to me after finding my name and three other coaches in the directory of the ICF web site. She said she wanted to review several options before deciding on the best fit for her. In our introductory session, she outlined four goals and they were quite varied: (1) receive recognition as a team player at work, (2) do more community-based activities, (3) create a wellness plan for herself, (4) create financial well-being. After telling me her goals, she asked about how my coaching could help her meet these goals. First off, I told her what I noticed was how varied her interests were and asked if she wanted to focus on them equally. She said there was a priority on what to do first. I told her that coaching would hold her accountable to what she wanted to create and that I would mention each goal on every call and inquire, "What's next in this area?" We would also coach to any blocks that got in the way to her success and I would hold her vision as completely as possible even in times of her own doubt. We discussed how we might go about working together and I intentionally stressed her options regarding use of her time, as well as my varied coaching techniques and tools that I use according to her needs. She told me she planned to follow through on talking with all four prospective coaches and said she'd get back to me within two weeks. Within 10 days, Helen called and said, "When can we start?"

With Helen, I laid out the ICF core competencies as rich and varied guidelines for our coaching interactions. I shared the rowboat analogy, but this time focused more on our team aspect moving her life forward with each of us being a crucial team member to making it work. Where she became most challenged was in her tendency to allow her work to take her overall focus. The use of *Active Listening and Powerful Questions*, brought her the insight that she wasn't remembering her initial goals of coaching, but rather her work always got the attention in our calls. They were her request for coaching at the start of every session. She did get her desired results at work first, while she admitted over and over again that she knew the other areas weren't getting as much attention.

Her next step was to design small actions in each of the three other goal areas until she was ready to give them equal weight. Through six weeks of reminding her of her choice to put her job first, she gained results, but also saw how she controlled the results in her life. She began to bring in her financial project at the start of calls, followed by the community focus, and then wellness. She really got how she had been living her life out of balance and what her role was in having it be that way. At the conclusion of her four months of coaching, she had saved money in the bank, had adopted a community project, and was meditating and walking on her lunch breaks as a daily practice. Her work results improved as well as her attitude about her life.

IN CONCLUSION

It's critical for you as the coach to know your values so that you can decide what to do and not to do in a session. Otherwise your session will come from your values bias. Striving to lessen your bias assists your client in being who they are, to discover their strengths, and make changes to achieve better results.

As a Hub Motivational Value System, I am aware of my tendency to describe or narrate in a way that is not *cut and dry*. I catch myself and ask to start over, or simply take a moment to think of a logical sequence. I also have a tendency to question beyond what may be needed in the moment. With this knowledge of what I tend to "overdo" I am more aware of how I am delivering the coaching and readjust if it is not meeting the client's need.

This book itself has a value filter as well. It is the value of supporting the client to reach their end state. Some may say this is a Blue value. Others may say it is Red because you are paid to create a result. Others may say it is Green because you need to follow a process of the ICF Core Competencies. Whatever it is for you, practice what you've learned, and you'll move from providing coaching to providing *meaningful* coaching.

STRENGTH
DEPLOYMENT
INVENTORY
INTERPRETIVE GUIDE

The 7 Motivational Value Systems

Your Motivational Value System acts as an internal filter through which life is interpreted and understood. It is a unifying set of values for choosing behavior that enhances our sense of self-worth.

Blue: Altruistic–Nurturing

- *Concern for the protection, growth, and welfare of others*

Red: Assertive–Directing

- *Concern for task accomplishment*
- *Concern for organization of people, time, money and any other resources to achieve desired results*

Green: Analytic–Autonomizing

- *Concern for assurance that things have been properly thought out*
- *Concern for meaningful order being established and maintained*

Hub: Flexible–Cohering

- *Concern for flexibility*
- *Concern for members of the group and the welfare of the group*
- *Concern for belonging in the group*

Red-Blue: Assertive–Nurturing

- *Concern for the protection, growth, and welfare of others through task accomplishment and leadership*

Red-Green: Judicious–Competing

- *Concern for intelligent assertiveness, justice, leadership, order, and fairness in competition*

Blue-Green: Cautious–Supporting

- *Concern for affirming and developing self-sufficiency in self and others*
- *Concern for thoughtful helpfulness with regard for justice*

Understanding Conflict

Your Conflict Sequence describes internal changes in feelings and motives in response to perceived threats. While people most frequently use behavior that looks very similar to they way they are feeling, other behavior choices are always available.

Internal Experience in Conflict

Conflict Stage	Focus is on:	BLUE	RED	GREEN
Stage 1	Self Problem Other	Simply being accommodating to the needs of others.	Simply rising to the challenge being offered.	Simply being prudently cautious.
Stage 2	Self Problem ~~Other~~	Giving in and letting the opposition have its way.	Having to fight off the opposition.	Trying to escape from the opposition.
Stage 3	Self ~~Problem~~ ~~Other~~	Having been completely defeated.	Having to fight for one's life.	Having to retreat completely.

Observable Behavior in Conflict

Conflict Stage	BLUE	RED	GREEN
Stage 1	Accommodate others	Rise to the challenge	Be prudently cautious
Stage 2	Surrender conditionally	Fight to win	Pull back and analyze
Stage 3	Surrender completely	Fight for survival	Withdraw

Managing Your Strengths

Any strength can be overdone, or perceived as overdone by another person. The table below is condensed from the SDI. It lists some strengths of four Motivational Value Systems that can be productive in a coaching relationship, but unproductive in the same relationship if they are overdone.

Blue: Altruistic-Nurturing

Characteristic Strength:	If Overdone Can Become...
Helpful	Smothering
Caring	Submissive
Supportive	Self-sacrificing

Red: Assertive-Directing

Characteristic Strength:	If Overdone Can Become...
Forceful	Dictatorial
Quick to act	Rash
Competitive	Combative

Green: Analytic-Autonomizing

Characteristic Strength:	If Overdone Can Become...
Methodical	Rigid
Analytical	Nit picking
Principled	Unbending

Hub: Flexible-Cohering

Characteristic Strength:	If Overdone Can Become...
Flexible	Wishy washy
Open to change	Inconsistent
Experimenter	Aimless

CLIENT PREPARATION SHEET

Client Preparation Sheet

What are your values?

_____

_____

_____

What behaviors do you tend to overdo?

_____

_____

_____

What are values of your client?

_____

_____

_____

What will you do more of with this client?

_____

_____

_____

What will you do less of with this client?

_____

_____

_____

Which of the ICF core competencies do you want to strengthen?

_____

_____

_____

    I. Meeting Ethical Guidelines and
        Professional Standards   _____

    II. Establishing The Coaching Agreement _____

    III. Establishing Trust and Intimacy
         With The Client   _____

    IV. Coaching Presence _____

    V. Active Listening _____

    VI. Powerful Questioning _____

    VII. Direct Communication _____

    VIII. Creating Awareness _____

    IX. Designing Actions _____

    X. Planning and Goal Setting _____

    XI. Managing Progress and Accountability _____

REFERENCES

Frankl, V. E. (1959). *Man's Search for Meaning*. New York: Simon & Schuster.

Frankl, V. E. (1986). *The Doctor and the Soul*. New York: Vintage Books.

Scudder, T. (2009). *Strength Deployment Inventory Facilitation Guide*, 4th Edition. Carlsbad: Personal Strengths Publishing.

International Coach Federation, www.coachfederation.org

Personal Strengths Publishing, www.personalstrengths.com

ABOUT THE AUTHOR

Tina Mertel has been in leadership development since 1991, working with organizations and individuals to improve their performance. In addition to her coaching practice, she is a Master Facilitator of the Strength Deployment Inventory, certifying new facilitators in the use of the methodology.

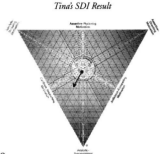

Tina's SDI Result

She received a Bachelor of Science degree in Business Administration, and a Master of Arts degree with Distinction in Human Behavior. She is an Associate Certified Coach with the ICF, and has served as a Mentor Coach with an ICF-accredited Coach Training Program. Awards include: the Distinguished Service Award from the American Society of Training and Development (ASTD), Advanced Toastmaster (ATM), and placing first in a national writing contest on the Adult Student in Society.

Tina has lived in a variety of areas throughout the world. As a first-generation American, she honors the nuances of merging cultures whether they stem from various countries, families, or organizational dynamics.

With a sense of adventure and heart, Tina's training and coaching focus on the possibilities for change and innovation with an eye on what is truly most important for her client.